SPOTTED OWLS

JARED HOBBS

text by Richard Cannings

foreword by Eric Forsman

SPOTTED Owls

Shadows in an Old-Growth Forest

GREYSTONE BOOKS
DOUGLAS & McINTYRE PUBLISHING GROUP
Vancouver/Toronto/Berkeley

07 08 09 10 11   5 4 3 2 1

Greystone Books
A division of Douglas & McIntyre Ltd.
2323 Quebec Street, Suite 201
Vancouver, British Columbia
Canada V5T 4S7
www.greystonebooks.com

Library and Archives Canada Cataloguing in Publication
Hobbs, Jared, 1971–
Spotted owls : shadows in an old-growth forest /
Jared Hobbs ; text by Richard Cannings.

Includes index.
ISBN 978-1-55365-241-0

1. Spotted owl. 2. Rare birds.
I. Cannings, Richard J. (Richard James) II. Title.
QL696.S83H62 2007   598.9′7   C2007-901826-2

Editing by Nancy Flight
Design by Jessica Sullivan and Naomi MacDougall
Jacket photograph by Jared Hobbs
Printed and bound in China by C & C Offset Printing Co., Ltd.
Printed on paper that comes from sustainable forests
managed under the Forest Stewardship Council.
Distributed in the U.S. by Publishers Group West

We gratefully acknowledge the financial support
of the Canada Council for the Arts, the British Columbia
Arts Council, the Province of British Columbia through
the Book Publishing Tax Credit, and the Government of
Canada through the Book Publishing Industry Development
Program (BPIDP) for our publishing activities.

This book is dedicated to the owls for accepting me

into their mysterious and secretive nocturnal world

and allowing me to photograph their elusive ways.

Contents

Foreword

NO OWL HAS INSPIRED as much interest and controversy

as the Spotted Owl. During the last thirty years, it has been

intensively studied and has been the subject of numerous court

cases in which federal agencies, environmental groups, and for-

est industry groups have fought over how to manage the owl

and the forests in which it lives. This debate has brought about

huge changes in public perception of the owls and in the philos-

ophy of forest management in North America. As someone

who has been involved in this debate for over thirty years, I find these changes nothing short of amazing. At the same time, I am often disheartened by the tidal wave of humanity that makes it increasingly difficult to protect species like the Spotted Owl. I know I am not alone in this feeling.

For many people, the Spotted Owl has become a symbol. Like bison and wolves on the Prairies, whales in the oceans, and polar bears on Arctic ice floes, Spotted Owls have become symbols of the wild places and wild things that are gradually disappearing as humans intrude into every corner of the earth. As one of the most unusual and charismatic species in the rugged mountains of western North America, the Spotted Owl has also become an emblem of the massive global wave of extinction that is occurring as a result of climate change and human modification of habitats.

Unlike most other large owls, Spotted Owls have little fear of humans and often fly in to get a closer look at human visitors to their remote forest world. Because they are so approachable and at the same time so mysterious,

A Mexican Spotted Owl peers through the maple leaves.

Spotted Owls are dutiful parents and tend closely to their young throughout their development.

they have been studied by large numbers of scientists and have been written about by many journalists and college students and even schoolchildren. Spotted Owls are also highly adapted to living in dense forests and steep canyons, where they prey on nocturnal mammals such as flying squirrels, woodrats, and tree voles. This specialization makes them sensitive to changes in their forest environment, and the evidence from the meticulous work of researchers suggests that the owls' numbers have gradually declined as their habitat has dwindled.

My first encounter with a Spotted Owl, in the middle of the night in the mountains of western Oregon over thirty years ago, led to a lifetime spent studying this elusive species. It is difficult to put into words why I find it so intriguing, but many others have also succumbed to the allure of this beautiful and soulful creature of the night. The photographs and the words in this book are testimony to that allure.

Jared Hobbs's infatuation with Spotted Owls began in 1997, after his first encounter with a Spotted Owl one spring evening near Pemberton, British Columbia. That night his journey to capture, on film, the magic of this owl began with a commitment to produce a book, a visual celebration of the

4 }

owl, to share with those who cared to learn more. Over the next decade, he travelled frequently to Washington, Oregon, California, and Arizona, where Spotted Owls were more plentiful, to capture the images for this book.

In 2004 Jared was assigned the job of documenting the status of the Spotted Owl in British Columbia. This was no easy task, because Spotted Owls have never been very common in British Columbia, and they have become decidedly less so as their habitat has been logged and as the Barred Owl, a close relative, has gradually invaded the province. By 2002 the B.C. population was estimated at only about thirty pairs. Jared set out to provide a more accurate estimate by surveying all of the remaining owl habitat, including the more remote, previously unsurveyed areas deep within British Columbia's parks and protected areas. Such a survey had never been undertaken before. As a result of this survey, we now know that there are only a few pairs remaining in British Columbia, sheltered primarily in protected park areas that have not been logged.

This book is the culmination of Jared's photographic odyssey into the world of the Spotted Owl. In many ways his pictures speak much more eloquently about the owl and the places where it lives than words can ever do. I hope this book will inspire people to become involved citizens and to advocate for the protection of all species with which we share this earth.

Eric Forsman
Wildlife Biologist

Photographer's

PREFACE

MY INVOLVEMENT WITH Spotted Owls began in the early

1990s, when I read a paper by Eric Forsman for a university

assignment. I was instantly captivated, and after graduation I

applied for a job assisting with inventories of Spotted Owls in

British Columbia.

It was during my first week in this position, in 1997, that

I finally got to see my first Spotted Owl. We were surveying a

known site, using a tape-recorded call in hopes of determining

whether the owl was still occupying its territory. A little after 10 PM we heard a response from the owl. My heart began to race. She wasn't far from the road, and I could tell from her calls that she was approaching. Suddenly she appeared, and I watched as her silhouette drifted silently across the road in front of me before alighting noiselessly on a branch just a few metres away. When she turned to look at me, I could see into her eyes in the light of the moon. I watched her, spellbound, until she silently slipped back to her nocturnal forest world.

After looking into the owl's eyes, I knew that only photographs could convey the soulful look of wisdom I had seen. That night I committed myself to what would become a ten-year goal to produce a book about this alluring owl. Had I known in advance what would be involved, I would have felt overwhelmed. But in ignorance I proceeded.

At the end of that summer, I invested my earnings in some camera gear and used what money was left to travel to the old-growth forests from

British Columbia to Mexico as often as I could to photograph these owls again and again. My work as a biologist led me elsewhere for a while, but I continued to seek out and photograph Spotted Owls throughout their range. I also continued to read about Spotted Owls. By necessity, my efficiency in finding Spotted Owls quickly improved, and by 2002 I was working as a Spotted Owl biologist. I quickly became heavily involved in Spotted Owl research in British Columbia, leading inventory efforts and conducting telemetric monitoring of dispersing juvenile owls, to better inform management efforts in Canada.

Exactly a decade after my first encounter with a Spotted Owl, and after countless days and nights spent hiking up steep mountainsides with heavy camera gear, I finally had the images I needed to tell the story of this magical owl. These are the images you will see in this book. I hope that they convey the beauty of this owl and the tragedy of its decline.

‹ Early explorers referred to this species as the "Canyon Owl," once commonly found in wooded canyons throughout its range.

Introduction

IN THE LATE 1960s, little was known about owls. Birders and biologists tended to explore forests during the day rather than at night and encountered owls more by accident than by design. The Spotted Owl was no exception to this rule. Not only was it a night bird, but it lived in dense forests and remote canyons. Biologists considered it an uncommon owl throughout much of the West, from the coastal rain forests of British Columbia south to the pine-oak woodlands of the Sierra

Madre of Mexico. A few nests had been found, numbered specimens lay in drawers in vertebrate museums, and some lucky or more adventurous birders had it on their life lists. Most people in North America had never heard of it.

In 1968 a young biologist heard a Spotted Owl calling in the dark forests of Oregon. Eric Forsman became fascinated by the owl and quickly found out how little was known about it. He decided to study the Spotted Owl for his master's thesis in the early 1970s. After a few years of methodical surveys and countless hours on the biological night shift, he found that 95 percent of the Spotted Owls in his study area lived in old-growth forests. He also knew that industrial logging was eliminating these older forests at an alarming rate and that the young forests that replaced them would be harvested before they had developed the characteristics needed by the owls. His findings precipitated an avalanche of research projects, legislation, and legal battles. The Spotted Owl became a symbol of disappearing rain forests and galvanized a generation of environmentalists. By the 1990s the Spotted Owl was one of the best-studied owls in the world, and almost everyone in North America was well aware of its existence.

ORIGIN OF THE SPECIES

At first glance, the Spotted Owl appears to be a rather unassuming owl. It is less than half the size of the Great Horned Owl, which dominates the night skies across most of North America, but weighs almost twice as much as the

The aptly named Spotted Owl has a spotted head, back, chest, and belly.

Barred Owls have vertical streaks on their bellies and lack the pronounced white moustachial brow seen on Spotted Owls.

widespread Western Screech-Owl. It is the colour of rich chocolate, liberally speckled with white, especially below. Its round head lacks the earlike feather tufts typical of many forest owls, and its round face has deep brown, almost black eyes rather than the yellow ones common in the owl family. Like most owls, the Spotted Owl is more often heard than seen.

The commonest call heard from territorial Spotted Owls is a four-note series of high barks. A pair often calls back and forth to each other with this call during the breeding season, mostly at dusk and dawn. When the pair is agitated during a territorial dispute with other owls, the number of barks can be extended to ten or more. The other distinctive call heard from Spotted Owls is a loud, up-slurred whistle—*coooweep!*—which sounds uncannily like someone whistling for his or her dog. This is a contact call given most often by females.

Although it seems average in every respect, the Spotted Owl has a fascinating story to tell, a story that can teach humans important things about our own species and our relationship with the world. The beginnings of the story are still a matter of debate. The Spotted Owl closely resembles the Barred Owl, a slightly larger and paler species restricted until recently to eastern North America. The Barred Owl has the

same round head and dark eyes, but its belly feathers have vertical white and brown stripes instead of white spots. The call of the Barred Owl, though longer, deeper, and more raucous, has the same syncopated cadence as that of the Spotted Owl.

It would be easy to surmise that these two forest species, like many east-west pairs of North American birds, split from a shared ancestor during the Pleistocene ice ages, when glaciers overran the northern forests and southern populations were widely separated for millennia by the barren central plains. But recent genetic evidence suggests that the story is more complicated than that. Spotted and Barred owls are apparently only distantly related, the Barred Owl being closer to several tropical species in Central and South America than it is to its temperate cousin.

The climatic cycles over the two million years of the Pleistocene did change the Spotted Owl itself, though. As successive waves of ice forced bird populations south, the Spotted Owl found refuge in different forested regions. One refuge was likely the pine-oak forests of Mexico and the adjacent United States, woodlands that blanketed the central plateaus and clung to the rocky ridges of the Sierra Madre; a second refuge was the more coastal

Broadleaf trees, such as this alder, grow beneath the old-growth forest canopy and provide cover for roosting owls.

forests of California and Oregon. All these forests were cooler, wetter, and more extensive during the periods of glacial advance than they are today. Although the details may never be known, the populations of Spotted Owls living in these two regions gradually became different from one another as they adapted to the local environments.

These different populations are now considered three subspecies: the Northern Spotted Owl in the Cascades and Coast mountains from British Columbia south to central coastal California, the California Spotted Owl in the Sierra Nevada and other isolated ranges south to Baja California, and the Mexican Spotted Owl in more interior ranges from Utah and Colorado south to central Mexico. The Northern Spotted Owl is the largest and darkest of the three; the Mexican is the smallest and palest. The California Spotted Owl is intermediate in size and colour but closest to the Northern in behaviour and habitat selection. Those two subspecies meet in the Klamath region along the Oregon-California border, but interbreeding is minimal and they maintain genetic distinctions. The Mexican Spotted Owl is isolated geographically from the other two subspecies, but recent studies suggest that it is essentially identical genetically to the California Spotted Owl.

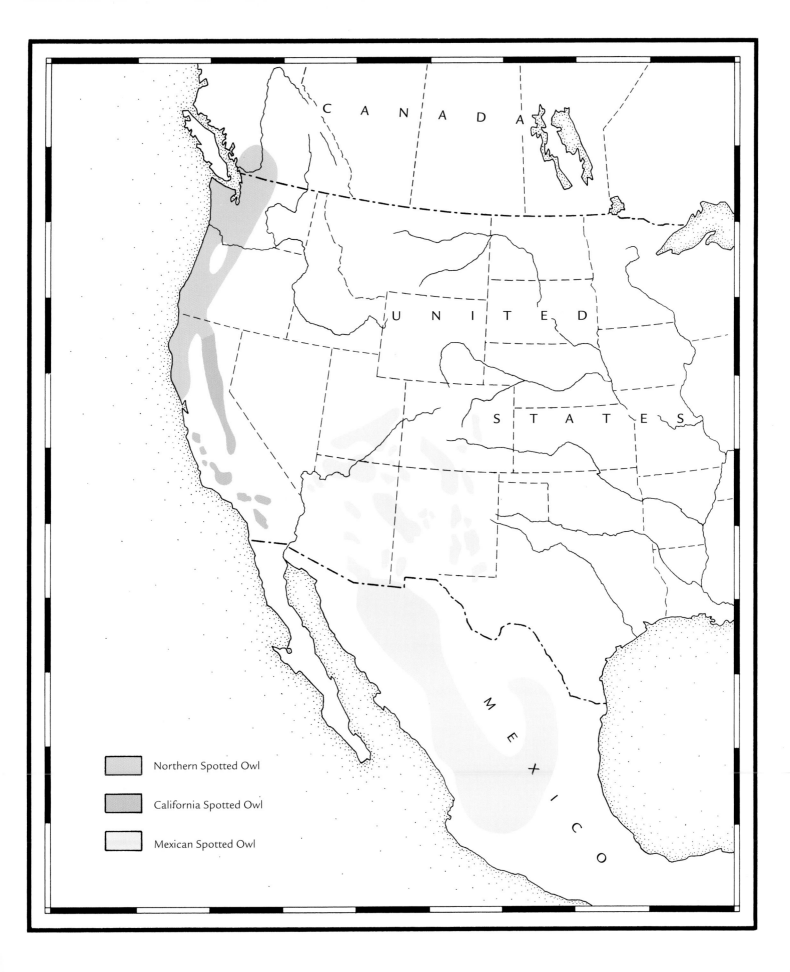

CANADA

UNITED

STATES

MEXICO

Northern Spotted Owl

California Spotted Owl

Mexican Spotted Owl

FORM AND FUNCTION

Like most owls, the Spotted Owl is a nocturnal predator, and everything about its form is adapted to that purpose. It has long, sharp talons to dispatch and hold prey and a strong, hooked beak to tear the bodies of its prey into pieces that it can swallow. Its plumage is cryptic, designed to blend into the shadows of the forest understory so that the owl can sleep peacefully during the day, undetected by larger predators or smaller birds that would disturb its rest.

The Spotted Owl finds its prey primarily by hearing, and it has the ears for the job. Its big, round face is a complex assemblage of feathers that gathers sound like a parabolic microphone, funneling it into large ear openings on each side of the face. Owl ears are unlike any others in the bird world, and not just because of their size. Many species, the Spotted Owl included, have asymmetrical ears, meaning that the right ear is a different size and shape from the left. In some species, such as the Boreal Owl, this asymmetry is built right into the skull, whereas in the Spotted Owl and its relatives it is restricted to the fleshy part of the ear opening. But the function is the same—the asymmetrical shape of the ears allows the owls to pinpoint the location of any sound in three-dimensional space.

The large, dark eyes of the Spotted Owl are also key to its success as a night hunter. Owl eyes are supremely adapted to low-light conditions, with round lenses set close to the retinas to maximize light gathering. Like cameras operating in low-light situations, the owls obtain this sensitivity at a cost, however—the resolution of their eyes is rather poor. They can see large objects very well at light levels in which we would be bumping into telephone poles without seeing them, but they lack the detailed vision that allows hawks and eagles to spot mice at great distances.

Some owls, such as the Barn Owl, find their prey by coursing back and forth over fields all night, but the Spotted Owl is a sit-and-wait predator. Its strategy is to perch silently in the forest and listen intently. If it hears the scratching of woodrat toenails on a log or the *thwack* of a flying squirrel landing on a tree trunk, it launches itself towards the sound, homing in on the prey with the accuracy of a laser-guided missile. The special structure of the owl's leading flight feathers and the velvety texture of all the wing feathers ensure that the Spotted Owl's flight is

‹ TOP: The serrated edges and finely textured surface of its wing feathers are part of the secret of the owl's silent flight. BOTTOM: The owl's razor-sharp talons and vice-like grip are formidable tools for catching prey.

⌄ Feathers at the edge of the owl's facial disk form a parabolic dish that channels sound towards its ear openings.

This female hunter prepares to seize an
unsuspecting mouse from the tip of a branch.

The Barn Owl, which can hunt entirely by sound,
is said to have the best hearing capabilities of
all the owls.

silent. This silence is needed so that owl will be able to hear the mouse while flying towards it and not be distracted by the sound of its own flapping wings.

The Spotted Owl has another interesting characteristic, which it shares with almost all other raptorial birds, something that has nothing to do with sharp talons and beaks. The female is considerably larger than the male; females weigh about 625 grams and male about 550 grams. The reason for this reversed sexual dimorphism, as biologists call it, has been the subject of great debate for decades. It is almost surely linked to the strong division of labour in hawks, eagles, and owls. In these species, the female performs all the nest duties, such as incubation of the eggs and brooding of the young, while the male does almost all the hunting for the family. Perhaps the small size of the male allows him to eat less of the prey he catches so that he can pass more on to the growing family, or maybe it makes him more agile so that he can catch flying and jumping prey more easily. Or maybe the female needs to be larger to produce and incubate a large clutch of eggs more easily. The theories are almost endless.

As in all species, the structure and behaviour of the Spotted Owl is the result of millennia of evolution and interaction with its environment. Being a predator near the top of the food chain, it is perhaps more sensitive to changes in that environment than other species.

‹ A juvenile clings to a mouse, while the
mother owl perches next to it, providing
protection for her offspring.

The World

OF THE SPOTTED OWL

HABITAT

The Spotted Owl is a forest bird, adapted to hunt, sleep, and

nest in extensive stands of large trees. The habitats it uses

differ tremendously from one end of its range to the other,

but it always avoids treeless areas, dislikes dense, young for-

ests, and prefers sites with significant amounts of older

forest. These older forests have a closed canopy but more open

understory and harbour a great diversity of plant species and tree sizes. Huge trees tower over small clearings formed by recent treefalls, and dead trees stand for decades as snags, slowly decaying while feeding and sheltering a huge variety of animals. After the snags fall, they become nurselogs, providing homes for everything from ants and mice to salamanders and wolverines, and young trees sprout from their decaying heartwood, nourished by the water and nutrients retained in the logs.

These old forests are ideal for Spotted Owls, perhaps most obviously because they contain an abundance of potential nest sites. Owls do not build nests—they must find ready-made sites that provide the necessary support and cover for their eggs and young. Spotted Owls generally look for large cavities in dead or dying trees. Sometimes they find suitable nests where a large branch has broken off and decay has carved into the trunk itself. A "stovepipe," the hollow at the top of a huge tree where the crown has snapped off in high wind, is another favourite site. Not only must the trees supporting these cavity sites be old, with some internal decay, they must also be large—their trunks are typically greater than 50 centimetres (almost 2 feet) in diameter. Spotted Owls will also take over the stick platform nests built by Northern Goshawks and Cooper's Hawks, species that are also typical of older, more open forests.

Another beneficial feature of these forests is the open, diverse character of their

understory. It is difficult to catch prey when flying through a dense, second-growth forest in the dead of night; it is much easier to swoop between the widely spaced trees in an older forest. There also tends to be a higher diversity and abundance of prey in older forests. The forest cannot be too open, however. Partially logged or naturally open stands with very low tree densities cannot provide the stable microclimate needed by roosting owls. Spotted Owls need to remain cool during hot days, so they perch near the ground in a shaded forest. During cold, wet weather the owls roost higher in the trees, still protected by the canopy but above the layer of cold air near ground level. Areas with scattered trees are also the preferred hunting habitat of the Great Horned Owl, a large predator that will happily consume a Spotted Owl whenever it has the opportunity.

Mexican Spotted Owls live in pine-oak forests from the southern Rocky Mountains to the central Sierra Madre. These are relatively dry forests that are naturally more open than the coastal forests of the Pacific Northwest. Spotted Owls choose the densest parts of the woods, where tall veteran pines mix with ancient oaks. Spotted Owl territories in these forests overlap those of Great Horned Owls, but the latter species uses the open meadows in the forests while the Spotted Owls stay under cover in the pines and oaks.

In southern Arizona and New Mexico, the mountains break up into small ranges that dot the desert plains. Ranges such as the Huachucas, Chiricahuas, and Animas are clothed with coniferous forests at higher elevations and carved throughout with deep, cool canyons. The canyon bottoms are filled with groves of stately sycamores that wind along the small streams. The smooth, white bark and pale green leaves of the sycamores contrast with the dark green needles of big Douglas-firs and Apache pines, whose deep roots tap into water seeping down the rock faces and talus slopes of the canyons. The Spotted Owls use these canyons for cool roosting sites and often nest in caves cut into the shady rock walls.

Farther south, smaller mountain ranges coalesce into the Sierra Madre of Mexico. The pine forests of the Sierra Madre retain many bird species familiar to birders from farther north—Red Crossbills call overhead, White-breasted Nuthatches probe the furrowed bark, and Steller's Jays scream loudly at any intrusion. But a decidedly tropical theme is evident— bromeliads sprout from the trunks of the trees, flocks of parrots chatter by, and several species of colourful trogons snatch berries from the madrones. Spotted Owls make their home here, too, with scattered territories in the barrancas—deep wooded canyons—and older pine-oak forests.

The California subspecies of the Spotted Owl occupies a great range of habitats, from low-elevation mixed woodlands dominated by oaks to high-elevation conifer forests. As elsewhere, the critical feature is a closed-canopy forest with significant numbers of large, mature trees. Some California Spotted Owls formerly nested in caves on cliffs, but few, if any, of these sites are occupied today; most of the owls nest in broken trees, natural cavities, or large stick nests built by hawks. Extensive cottonwood forests along river bottoms once provided nesting and foraging habitat that connected the populations living in isolated mountain ranges in southern California, but these woodlands were reduced long ago to remnant woodlots that can no longer support Spotted Owls.

The Northern Spotted Owl is found from southwestern British Columbia south to San Francisco Bay. In the northern part of this range, Spotted Owls are found in old-growth stands of western hemlock, western red cedar, and Douglas-fir. This is the classic temperate rain forest. The huge trees are cloaked in cold mist most of the winter and put on phenomenal growth in the warm, sunny summers. Most of the low-elevation forests in this area were logged in the 1900s, and the vestiges of old growth that remain are scattered in a landscape of thick, young forests and urban sprawl. Some of the Spotted Owls remaining in British Columbia and northern Washington are found in higher-elevation forests, but this is simply because they are the last old groves remaining. If the original forest were intact, the owls would rather be in the lower parts of the broad valleys.

On the east slope of the Cascades, Spotted Owls live in forests of mixed ponderosa pine and Douglas-fir. Many of the mature Douglas-firs have large twiggy clumps called witch's brooms, caused by an infestation of dwarf mistletoe. Some of these clumps are solid enough to provide an ideal nest platform for Spotted Owls, and most of the pairs in this region use them. Because Douglas-fir mistletoe is rare on the west slope of the Cascades, the birds there use tree cavities instead—or maybe the cavities provide extra protection from the abundant rainfall. In Marin County, just north of San Francisco, Spotted Owls nest in more diverse forests, where large redwoods, Douglas-fir, and bishop pine are mixed with a significant number of oaks and other deciduous trees.

Just how much habitat a pair of Spotted Owl needs varies with the geography and history of the site, but the key factor is prey density. Home ranges are largest at the northern end of the range, probably because the owls there rely on flying squirrels, which are smaller and less common than the woodrats in more southern forests. In Marin County, which has a large number of dusky-footed woodrats, Spotted Owl breeding densities are remarkably high; some nests are less than a kilometer apart, and home ranges are small. Northern Spotted Owl home ranges average about 3400 hectares, dropping to 1800 hectares for the California Spotted Owl, and to only 800 hectares for the Mexican Spotted Owl. The size of any single home range is almost always dependent on the amount and configuration of old forests within the territory, since the birds don't so much need a certain amount of land as a certain amount of good habitat.

◁ Nesting adult males often tear the heads off
their prey before delivering the rest to their mate.

▽ The male checks nervously before delivering the
prey, reluctant to reveal its secret nest location.

PREY

Another obvious aspect of habitat quality for any species is the availability of food. Energetics studies have suggested that a Spotted Owl needs to eat about 11 percent of its own body weight each day, amounting to over 26 kilograms of prey each year. Where do the owls get that food? Luckily, owls provide biologists with an easy way to quantify what prey they are eating.

Whenever an owl swallows a mouse or another tasty morsel, its stomach quickly digests the fleshy part of the meal but cannot break down the fur, bones, or feathers. This part of the meal gets rolled and squeezed into an oval pellet that is coughed up before the owl has another meal. The bones in these pellets can be counted and identified, so biologists can tell not only what kinds of prey have been eaten but how many of each.

Tens of thousands of Spotted Owl pellets have been analyzed throughout their range, so biologists know a lot about their diet. One of the biggest sets of data about the Spotted Owl diet comes from studies over the past thirty years in Oregon and Washington that sorted through almost 24,000 prey items. That sample contained at least 131 kinds of prey, including 48 species of mammals, 41 species of birds, 3 species of reptiles, 1 species of frog, 1 species of crayfish, 1 species of scorpion, 2 species of snails, and 33 species of insects. That list is surprisingly diverse, but one

species stands out as the mainstay of the Spotted Owl diet in that area—over 40 percent of the prey items were northern flying squirrels.

Most people don't appreciate how common northern flying squirrels are. Unlike other squirrels, northern flying squirrels are decidedly nocturnal; although humans don't encounter them often, night-hunting owls do. Flying squirrels aren't quite so tied to older forests as the owls are but do need older trees with cavities for nesting. The squirrels also feed a lot on arboreal lichens in winter, and these lichens are much more common and diverse in older forests than in second growth. The northern limit of the Spotted Owl range may well be governed by a declining density of flying squirrels. Spotted Owl feeding territories become progressively larger near this northern limit, suggesting that there may be a point where the owls would need to cover too much ground to find enough squirrels to survive.

Vancouver Island provides an interesting illustration of the relationship between the Spotted Owl and its prey. This large island is separated from the Olympic Peninsula of Washington and the Lower Mainland of British Columbia by relatively narrow bodies of water. Dispersing Spotted Owls could fly to the island, where they would find some magnificent tracts of forest. Flying squirrels would have a more difficult time reaching Vancouver Island, however, and have never colonized it. No Spotted Owls have ever been seen on Vancouver Island, either, and the simplest explanation is the lack of flying squirrels.

Studies from other parts of the Spotted Owl range tell a similar story, though owl populations south of Oregon concentrate on other medium-sized rodents, the woodrats. Considering that a single flying squirrel is about one-sixth the body mass of a Spotted Owl, and a woodrat about a third, one can appreciate why both these animals are popular as prey. Spotted Owls likely prefer woodrats over flying squirrels when both are equally available, but woodrats become much less common in the northern part of the owl's range, particularly in wet coastal forests.

Three species of woodrats are important to the Spotted Owl. The dusky-footed woodrat is found from southern Oregon south through California and is a very important prey item for the California Spotted Owl as well as for southern populations of the Northern Spotted Owl. Dusky-footed woodrat populations are densest in riparian woodlands, often those with thick stands of young deciduous trees. This habitat contrasts strongly with the older coniferous groves associated with good Spotted Owl habitat, so a mix of these habitat types is often ideal for the owls. Dusky-footed woodrats build bulky stick homes, often at the base of trees, but they will nest in tree cavities as well.

The range of the Mexican woodrat matches that of the Mexican Spotted Owl and is a key component

of the owl's diet. These rodents live in rocky habitats, building their nests in crevices and small caves. The third species of woodrat important to the Spotted Owl is the bushy-tailed woodrat; it is found from Yukon south to northern New Mexico and the Sierra Nevada. It is uncommon in the rain forests of the Pacific Northwest but much more abundant in the drier forests on the east slope of the Cascades. Like the Mexican woodrat, it favours rocky areas such as cliffs and talus slopes, but it can also build its nest high in trees.

In coastal Oregon and northern California, Spotted Owls also eat a lot of tree voles. Most species of voles are found in the dank, long grass of meadows, but tree voles live high in conifers, eating needles. Their arboreal habits make them susceptible to hunting Spotted Owls, but their small size probably makes them less preferred as a meal.

In winter many small animals are hibernating and others are scurrying safely beneath a blanket of snow, so menu items for the owls can be in short supply. But in summer the prey list expands to include everything from large insects (wood-boring beetles are favoured in northern forests, Jerusalem crickets in southern California), snakes, and lizards to young hares and rabbits. Bats are occasionally chased down, and pocket-gophers can be caught if they venture above ground. Deer mice form a substantial part of the Spotted Owl diet in some places, but since they weigh only a tenth as much as a woodrat, they don't contribute as much to the owl's larder. For example, deer mice make up almost 40 percent of the numbers of prey taken by Spotted Owls in northern Arizona, but that amounts to less than 20 percent of the

total prey by weight. Conversely, woodrats make up less than 8 percent of the prey items in the same area, but that converts into almost 30 percent of the total weight of prey.

Biologists have calculated that single Spotted Owls in Oregon and Washington probably eat more than one hundred flying squirrels each year, and a pair with two young can eat almost three hundred. If an owl has a lucky day and catches surplus prey, it will often cache the extra mouse or squirrel for future use, hiding it under thick moss or tucking it beneath a fallen log.

COMPETITION AND PREDATION

Spotted Owls share their forest territories not only with prey species but also with other owls that could compete with them for that prey. The closest competitor in this sense is the Barred Owl, but the story of its recent encounter with the Spotted Owl is so complex and so fascinating that is told in a separate section later in this book.

The Great Horned Owl is the heaviest and most powerful of the forest owls of western North America and not only competes with the Spotted Owl for rodent prey but is likely its most important predator. Great Horned Owls are especially effective at catching and eating young Spotted Owls when the latter are dispersing through the more open habitats favoured by Great Horneds. The Great Horned Owl is more of a visual predator,

More than two-thirds of avian-caused mortalities on Spotted Owls have been attributed to Great Horned Owls.

This tiny Whiskered Screech-Owl looks fierce but it's really only threatening to insects.

shunning the dark forests and instead watching for mammals around meadows and rocky ridges. It prefers larger prey than that of the Spotted Owl, especially hares and rabbits.

The Long-eared Owl looks somewhat like a Great Horned Owl, with similar long feather tufts at the top of the head, but is smaller than the Spotted Owl. It is a mouse specialist, coursing over mountain meadows at night, listening for meadow voles in the thick grass below. Perhaps its most likely arena of competition with the Spotted Owl is nest sites, since both species can use the stick nests of hawks, mistletoe-clumps on Douglas-firs, and broken-off ponderosa pine snags for that purpose.

There are two species of screech-owl in the North American range of the Spotted Owl—the Western and the Whiskered. Both are much smaller owls than the Spotted Owl, weighing about 200 and 100 grams, respectively. The Western Screech-Owl is found throughout the Spotted Owl's range, whereas the Whiskered is restricted to evergreen oak woodlands from southern Arizona to Nicaragua. Neither would compete with Spotted Owls for prey in a serious way; the Western Screech-Owl is a generalist predator of mice, small birds, and insects, and the Whiskered Screech-Owl eats almost nothing but insects and other arthropods. Both of these small owls nest and often roost in tree cavities. An even

smaller relative of the screech-owls, the Flammulated Owl, is an insect specialist found in dry coniferous forests from southern British Columbia south to Central America.

The Spotted Owl's biggest competitor for deer mice is the small Northern Saw-whet Owl. This highly nocturnal owl hunts in a very similar manner to that of the Spotted Owl but prefers deer mice when they are available. Generally weighing less than 100 grams, it nests in woodpecker cavities, as do most other small forest owls. Even smaller is the Northern Pygmy-Owl, another species common throughout the range of the Spotted Owl. It is a daytime hunter, seeking diurnally active prey such as meadow voles and songbirds.

The Spotted Owl has only two significant predators—the Great Horned Owl and the Northern Goshawk. Both of these powerful raptors primarily target young Spotted Owls as they move through the forest, dispersing to new territories. These juvenile owls are especially vulnerable in open habitats such as clear-cuts, where they are easily seen. Because Spotted Owls tend to nest in tree cavities, caves, and other enclosed areas, their eggs and young are not often robbed by other animals, though ravens have been seen trying to steal owl eggs on at least one occasion. Spotted Owls are big and powerful enough to deter most other nest robbers. The fledglings are exposed to mammalian predators such as bears, lynx, and coyotes while they are learning to fly, but this period is very short and they are closely guarded by their parents at that time.

< Juvenile Saw-whet Owls were once thought to be a distinct species and were mistakenly identified as Richardson's Owls.

ʌ A black bear enjoys a spring salad of dandelions.

{ 43

Mist cloaks the forest ridges and drifts through the trees—a common scene in the owl's coastal rain forest ecosystems.

< A male Western Screech-Owl guards its nest in this cottonwood tree.

⌄ The Northern Pygmy-Owl, the second smallest owl within the Spotted Owl's range, clutches a mouse almost half its size.

{ 47

Pocket gophers are a potential prey item for the Mexican Spotted Owl.

A banded male Spotted Owl in British Columbia deftly catches a mouse with a silenced flight that defies belief.

‹ A pair of juvenile Mexican Spotted Owls
peer from a cliff ledge.

{ 51

⌄ The golden yellow petals of the tiger lily curl
back delicately to expose the plant's pollen.

⟩ As summer slips into fall, the forest colours turn.
Temperatures in the day are still pleasant, but the
cool nights hint at harder times ahead as winter
approaches.

⌃ Coyotes are secretive and are seldom
  seen in the owl's forested habitat.

> The trailing fronds of goat's-beard lichen
  are testament to the age of the forest in
  this owl's nest grove.

◁ The Northern Goshawk is a forest raptor that
specializes in hunting other birds—including the
Spotted Owl. (PHOTO: WAYNE LYNCH)

‹ A female Spotted Owl swoops down to catch her prey,
flaring her wing and tail feathers to slow her approach.

⌄ Mule deer are common in coastal forested habitats
throughout the range of the Northern Spotted Owl.

⌄ Geothermal hot springs flow into Sloquet Creek, near Pemberton, British Columbia.

› Northern Saw-whet Owls hide during the day in dense thickets and tangles of underbrush.

Common and widespread,
the Great Horned Owl is North
America's most powerful
nighttime avian hunter.

{ 63

‹ A male Mexican Spotted Owl guards
a nearby cliff nest in this sandstone canyon
in southern Arizona.

Spotted Owls

THROUGH THE SEASONS

THE SPOTTED OWL New Year occurs sometime in late February or early March. The misty dawns break earlier, cutting short the night hunting time but promising warmer days. The starry late-winter nights are punctuated by the monotonous piping whistles of male Northern Saw-whet Owls looking for mates. By day, Song Sparrows sing from streamside shrubbery, and salmonberry blossoms form pink buds on the cinnamon-coloured canes. Pairs of Spotted Owls, which have hunted and

In the spring, the male Spotted Owl presents food to the female.

A pair of owls in southern Oregon roost together, preening one another as part of their springtime courtship ritual.

roosted separately all winter, begin to roost close together. As the spring twilight lengthens, the female begins to call the male at dusk with her slurred contact whistle, inviting copulation. The male flies in, hooting softly, and brings the female courtship offerings—dead flying squirrels, woodrats, or other rodents.

Perching side by side, the male and female often preen each other as a sign of growing closeness. During the evening courtship rituals, the male often flies to the nest site and gives a series of soft hoots from the nest. The site is usually at a lower elevation within the owls' home range, in a large stand of old forest. As the wooing intensifies, the female flies to the nest and gives a similar series of calls.

One night in the last half of March or early April, the female settles into the nest and the breeding season begins in earnest. The female stops hunting entirely but continues to accept the food offered by the male. This food not only impresses the female and solidifies the pair bond but is essential to help the female gain the weight necessary to produce the eggs. Northern females lay only two eggs in a clutch (occasionally only one), but females from southern populations often lay three. The eggs are laid two or three days apart, and the female begins incubating them as soon as they appear. After she begins incubating, her mating solicitations dwindle, as does her appetite. Some females can weigh close to a kilogram while laying eggs, but they trim down to a more svelte 600 grams by the time the young fledge.

Once the pair's behaviour becomes centred on the nest site, its foraging range can shrink by two-thirds; in the northwest it drops from over 3000 hectares to about 1000 hectares on average. Some pairs in the southwestern United States use less than 200 hectares during the breeding season.

While the female is incubating the eggs, she leaves the nest only briefly each night, to defecate, cough up pellets, and accept food from the male. After thirty days of incubation, the first egg hatches. Because the female incubates each egg as soon as it is laid, the second egg won't hatch for another two or three days. The first young to hatch is therefore two or three days older than the second young, is larger through-out the nestling period, and tends to get fed first at each feeding as long as it is hungry. This age and size difference is particularly pronounced in broods of three young, when the age differ-ence between the first and third young can be as much as six days.

Asynchronous hatching is common in raptors and some other groups of birds. It is thought to provide an efficient way for pairs to reduce the size of their brood if prey become hard to find. If all three young were the same age and size, they would become equally mal-nourished—and all might die—if the male

A juvenile Northern Spotted Owl peers with trepidation into the world that awaits.

The female pauses before dropping into the nest to deliver prey to her young, hidden inside the chimney cavity.

could only bring in enough food to provide for one or two of them. But if one of the birds is larger, it will dominate the feedings and make sure it gets enough food to grow normally. The youngest may eventually starve, but at least one or two young will survive.

The young are born blind and helpless and covered in white down. Now that more food is needed by the family, the male brings prey more regularly. As he approaches the nest, he gives a series of hoots, usually muffled by a mouthful of rodent, to announce his arrival, and the female often replies with a contact whistle, telling him to make his delivery at the nest. If she is particularly anxious to get the food, she will fly from the nest to the male, giving a series of whimpering hoots. The small young chatter loudly, swaying back and forth with their mouths open, when the female offers them bits of food torn off prey items. At this young age, they chatter and open their mouths at any disturbance around the nest, assuming it means that a meal is on the way.

The young birds' eyes begin to open after about a week, and they almost immediately learn what their parents look like. After that they beg for food only when a parent arrives at the nest. The female continues to brood the young, keeping them warm, until they are big enough and their feathers

⟨ When the owls first leave the nest, they are little more than fluffy balls of down with a few primary flight feathers.

⌄ By July the stiff feathers that define the edge of the facial disk have begun to grow in.

developed enough that they can stay warm by themselves. As they grow, the female broods them less and less and helps the male hunt more and more. When the young are in such a rapid growth phase, the pair needs to catch as much prey as possible.

When the young are about two weeks old, their regular feathers begin to replace their white natal down. About this time the female begins to roost outside the nest for longer periods. Sometime in late May or June, when they are about five weeks old, the young leave the nest. They are still quite downy and can't fly properly at this stage; most fledglings make rather inglorious departures from the nest, crashing into bushes and hanging upside down from branches. They often spend several days on or near the ground until they build up the strength and coordination to climb or flutter back up onto nearby branches. If they are in steep terrain, they quickly learn to glide to trees downslope. Siblings tend to stay fairly close together at this time, and usually one of the adults roosts with them during the day.

By July the young are quite capable flyers and can follow the adults more as they look for prey. The adults can find the young easily through the summer nights; the hungry birds give out regular hissing shrieks that have a double meaning—

The juveniles spend their days preening their feathers and sleeping.

For a young owl like this one, regurgitating a cone-sized pellet of fur and bones can be quite a challenge.

here I am and *feed me*. The young can now process large food items on their own, ripping woodrats into bite-sized pieces. They start to practise catching prey, pouncing on flies or attacking clumps of moss, but are still totally reliant on the adults to catch their meals. More adult-looking feathers grow in through August, and the young gradually become more independent. By September they can take care of themselves, and the adults stop feeding them altogether. The young often fly after the adults in early September, hoping for one last free meal, but the beleaguered parent usually flies away. At last the young understand that they are on their own. At the same time, hormonal signals in their bodies urge them to move, and juvenile dispersal begins.

Sometime in the fall—September at the northern edge of the range, late October or November in the south—the juveniles leave their natal territories and strike out on their own to find a new home. They travel in random directions and cover large distances at first, sometimes more than 10 kilometers per night, but then they slow down to search for a suitable winter territory. A few juveniles travel more than 100 kilometers, but the great majority travel less than 50 kilometers; females tend to go farther than males.

The primary feature the owls are looking for in a new home is not so much a tract of empty old forest full of flying squirrels or woodrats as the

presence of other Spotted Owls. The presence of the older birds is a good clue for the youngster that this is good habitat, and the young bird may function as insurance for the older birds. If one of the adults dies, there's a better chance that a replacement mate is close at hand, and one that knows the territory as well. Young owls are tolerated in the territories of resident owls until they are three years of age. They then must leave the territory to find a mate.

In many parts of the species' range, particularly in the Pacific Northwest, young Spotted Owls must travel through large areas of unsuitable habitat before they settle down. They try to use older forests as much as possible, but many are forced to move through clear-cuts and young forests, where hunting is difficult and the prospects of finding another Spotted Owl are even slimmer. Every night spent in a cutover habitat increases the likelihood that they will be hunted by a Great Horned Owl, and at this time they are still very much novices in the art of catching rodents. Faced with starvation and a gauntlet of predators, most juveniles—between 67 and 100 percent, depending on the year and location—die during this dispersal phase.

Those that do survive to find a suitable home still have to face another challenge. Winter is a difficult time for Spotted Owls, especially at high elevations in the North Cascades, where snow fills the forests to depths unheard of elsewhere in the world. Along the coast, periods of prolonged rainfall reduce prey activity and make hunting more difficult. At this time even the resident pairs, no longer tied to the nest site, split up and roam a much wider territory to find enough food to get through the cold, wet days and nights. Home range size in the Pacific Northwest triples in winter to an average of 3400 hectares. In the Sierra Nevada, many Spotted Owls move well downslope in early winter, forsaking the high coniferous forests for the oak woodlands in the foothills, a vertical migration to find a winter home with less snow and more prey.

Some of the young birds move again in spring to look for another territory. Some pair up at one year of age, but very few of these young pairs breed. Most begin to breed at two to five years of age. Once they begin breeding, Spotted Owls remain true to their territory and their mates. Only a few abandon a site once they settle; these birds tend to be young, single females.

Spotted Owls have a characteristically low reproductive rate. Most pairs don't nest every year, and only a third to half of the pairs manage to successfully fledge at least one young each year. To make up for this low rate, the owls are rather long-lived. Annual survivorship of adults is greater than 80 percent, and many survive into their late teens. One captive female lived for more than thirty years.

‹ In winter the owl's food requirements
increase dramatically as it tries to maintain
a body temperature between 38 and 40°c.

{ 81

When Spotted Owls get wet they fan
out their feathers to increase ventilation
and water evaporation.

A tender moment of bonding between
the mother and her owlet.

After the owl's first flight from the nest, it will often sit on the ground for a while before climbing to a safe perch.

Chimney nests such as this one take hundreds of years to form.

A pair of juvenile Spotted Owls gets ready to leave the nest in mid-June.

The rapidly growing juveniles require several "mice-sized" meals every day to meet their growth needs.

By early August, wing feathers are fully formed and the feathers that define the edge of the facial disk have grown in.

A fallen maple leaf creates an appealing pattern
against the river stones.

A young Great Horned Owl has just fledged the nest.

‹ A mother delivers the remains of
a pack rat, retrieved from a nearby
cache site, to her young owlet.

⌄ Windblown snow coats the trunks of these giant
sequoias in Kings Sequoia National Park, California.

⌄ If something threatens the nest, the female will
spread her wings, in a behaviour known as "mantling,"
to hide her young.

This adult male Mexican Spotted Owl grooms lazily, using a shaded ravine to escape the Arizona heat.

A young male owl poses atop a small Douglas-fir stump in the late fall.

> The adults roost in close proximity to their young until the juveniles are capable of defending themselves.

‹ Mexican Spotted Owls are found in the forested mountaintops of Arizona, Colorado, New Mexico, and Mexico.

The Future

OF THE SPOTTED OWL

CURRENT CHALLENGES

Habitat loss and fragmentation Throughout its range, the Spotted Owl needs old forests to survive. Most of the forests in the West were logged throughout the 1900s; only about 5 to 10 percent of the original forests remain. The logged habitats range from recent clear-cuts to dense second-growth forests that lack most or all of the characteristics needed by the owls—abundant prey, adequate nest sites, protection from predators, and cool roost conditions.

Beams of sunlight pierce the still, dark depths of an ancient redwood rain forest near Arcata, California.

Barred owls are now thought to be the most common owl in western North America's coastal forests.

The old forest that remains is increasingly fragmented. Small stands of mature trees cling to steep slopes at the upper end of mountain valleys, separated from other suitable habitat by cutover watersheds, valleys of intensive agriculture, and seas of concrete and asphalt. Whole valleys with intact forests are extremely rare and are limited to the few large parks in the area. Forestry plans throughout the West call for the continued logging of most older forests, with no plans to allow second-growth forests to grow back into a mature state in any significant amounts before reharvesting.

Detailed studies of Spotted Owl ecology—and there have been many—show that the area needed by a pair of owls increases dramatically in fragmented forests. Landscapes with less than 20 percent old forest cannot support Spotted Owls, and that figure is likely higher toward the northern edge of the species' range, in Washington and British Columbia. Conversely, the abundance and productivity of Spotted Owls increase with increasing proportions of old forest.

The Barred Owl The misfortunes of the Spotted Owl at the hands of humans over the past century have been aggravated in the last few decades by pressures from its big cousin, the Barred Owl. Barred and Spotted owls have lived largely separately for millennia, the Barred Owl confined mainly to hardwood and

mixed forests in eastern North America and the Spotted Owl in coniferous forests in the West. Their ranges overlapped only in the pine-oak woodlands of Mexico. The two species still meet in Mexico but likely have never competed significantly there. The Barred Owl subspecies of Mexico is the largest of the species, whereas the Mexican Spotted Owl is the smallest of its species, so the considerable size difference between the species is amplified there.

Historically, the Barred Owl was found north to Ontario and southeastern Manitoba; its western limit was likely checked by the frigid winters and short summers of the continental interior and the wide expanse of the prairies. But in the mid-1800s the world's climate began to warm significantly as the globe emerged from the four-century-long Little Ice Age. As temperatures ameliorated, Barred Owls began to move west through the forests that formed the northern border of the Great Plains; they were first seen in Alberta in 1934. When they reached northeastern British Columbia in the early 1940s, they turned south into some of the most productive forests on the continent. By the mid-1960s the first pioneers crossed the border into Washington, and the species reached Oregon in 1974 and California in 1981.

Barred Owls negatively affect populations of several indigenous owl species as they expand their range in North America.

It's easy for those not familiar with owls to confuse the spotted back of a Barred Owl with that of a Spotted Owl.

The Barred Owl is more of an ecological generalist than the Spotted Owl. It needs a few big old trees in which to nest and roost but forages successfully in many types of forests. It is also more of a generalist when it comes to food; the list of prey species it takes is similar to that of the Spotted Owl, but it doesn't rely on flying squirrels and woodrats to the same extent. The changing western landscapes of the late 1900s that fueled the decline of the Spotted Owl were more than adequate to sustain the new population of Barred Owls. A total of seven hundred Barred Owl territories have been found in Oregon since the species arrived in 1974, and new territories sprang up there at an average of sixty per year through the 1990s.

The arrival of the Barred Owl irrevocably changed the Spotted Owl neighbourhood. Although the new birds were bigger and more aggressive, they rarely muscled their way into an occupied territory and evicted the Spotted Owl tenants. But they did quickly take over any suitable territory that became vacant, and once a territory has switched to Barred Owls, it is very unlikely to be occupied by Spotted Owls. In the animal world, as in the human world, possession is nine-tenths of the law.

Barred Owls are affecting the Spotted Owl through another, perhaps more insidious threat—hybridization. Although hybridization

The white moustachial brow is a reliable identifying feature and distinguishes a purebred Spotted Owl from a hybrid.

Crossbreeding between Spotted and Barred owls is unusual; biologists refer to these hybrids as "Sparred Owls."

between two species is rather uncommon in nature, it can occur with surprising regularity when one of the species is so rare that individuals have difficulty locating mates of their own species. The advance of the Barred Owl into the fragmented landscape of declining Spotted Owl populations has produced just such a circumstance.

Beginning in 1986, owls that were clearly hybrids between Spotted and Barred owls were discovered in Washington, and similar individuals have since been seen and studied in Oregon and British Columbia as well. These birds are intermediate in plumage and size and give aberrant calls. Hybrid birds readily pair and mate with both Barred and Spotted owls; the progeny of these pairs are very difficult to distinguish as hybrids, since they resemble their pure parent. Most hybrids seem to pair with Barred Owls, leading to concerns that the Barred Owl may overwhelm the small Spotted Owl population through hybridization, since the subsequent hybrids would be more and more like Barred Owls with each generation. Male hybrids seem to be fully fertile, but because of chromosomal processes female hybrids produce very few young.

Fire The combined threats of habitat loss and Barred Owls are clearly having a significant impact on Spotted Owl populations in the northern part of their range. All populations,

especially those in the southern and northeastern parts of the range, are vulnerable to a third major threat—wildfire. For the past century, the natural forest fire regime across western North America has been radically altered. In drier forest types, indigenous peoples once set fires regularly, maintaining older, fire-resistant trees and removing smaller trees and shrubs. Not only has that practice stopped, but in the mid-1990s forest managers undertook the opposite strategy of forest fire suppression, spearheaded by Smokey the Bear.

Fire suppression has created large buildups in the fuel load of forests—thick growths of underbrush and accumulations of dead branches. As a result, although fire suppression stops the spread of many small fires, it promotes the intensity of fires that grow out of control. These firestorms destroy huge areas of forest throughout the West each year. Recent fires in southern California have burned large tracts of Spotted Owl habitat. Rectifying this situation is complex; forests are thinned through selective logging, and then a more regular fire regime is restored with purposely set fires. Both these actions may result in habitats that are more open than is optimal for Spotted Owls. However, recent studies in Arizona and New Mexico found that fires set by forest managers to create a more open forest understory had little effect on Spotted Owl distribution.

{ 109

THE VIEW AHEAD

Much has happened since Eric Forsman began his research on Spotted Owls in the 1970s. The species' plight has been widely recognized; the Spotted

> This male Spotted Owl takes advantage
  of an opportunity to catch an unsuspecting
  mouse during the day.

Owl was listed as Endangered in Canada in 1986. The U.S. government followed suit, listing the Northern Spotted Owl as Threatened in 1990 and the Mexican Spotted Owl as Threatened in 1993. A petition to list the California Spotted Owl was turned down in 2006, an action already being criticized because it did not take into account new forestry plans that would log Spotted Owl habitat.

These listings have prompted a plethora of management plans designed to protect the owl while still allowing logging across its range. Most of these plans were shelved during years of litigation, and many that have been enacted have been focused on the short-term viability of forestry companies rather than the long-term viability of the owl. In fact, the recovery plan for the Northern Spotted Owl was the first recovery plan written by the United States Fish and Wildlife Service that proposed a population goal smaller than the present, already threatened population. That plan has, however, resulted in the preservation of about 80 percent of older forests in Washington and Oregon in some sort of reserve status, but elsewhere this flurry of action around the Spotted Owl has resulted in an astonishing amount of inaction in conserving both the owl and the old forest ecosystem it has come to symbolize.

The Spotted Owl population continues to dwindle across its range. The Canadian population was estimated at 100 pairs in 1990, down from a historical estimate of 500 pairs. By 2000 there were fewer than 50 pairs in Canada, and in 2006 there were only 3 known pairs. Only one of those pairs

bred successfully that year. The obvious cause for the declining Canadian population is that essentially no young birds are surviving to breeding age. The remaining birds are all old and near the end of their reproductive lives.

The total Northern Spotted Owl population is estimated to be less than 5000 pairs, the California Spotted Owl population 1500 pairs, and the Mexican Spotted Owl population 1500 pairs. That may seem like a healthy number of owls, but the numbers are declining steadily in almost every population. Overall, the population seems to be declining at about 4 percent per year; if that rate continues, the population will drop by 50 percent over the next fifty years. What is more worrisome is that detailed field studies show a decline in the survival rates of adult females, and in some areas that decline is accelerating. In a long-lived species, declining survivorship of adult females can lead to rapid and long-lasting population declines.

Eric Forsman's findings were a wake-up call that all was not well in the forests of northwestern North America The alarms it set off changed the course of forest and wildlife management across North America. Biologists quickly realized that the declining numbers of Spotted Owls were not just a symptom of malaise within that species but a sign that the ecosystem itself was unraveling, changing into something different.

Unfortunately, the debate in public and political circles still centres on owls versus humans—should we give up some forestry jobs for the sake of another species? These debates all too frequently ignore the fact that the forestry industry was in decline long before the owls came into the picture. That in itself should have awakened us to the fact that our forests cannot withstand such high and prolonged rates of harvest. As a society, we must learn, and learn quickly, that the maintenance of healthy ecosystems around us is essential for our quality of life and, ultimately, for our own survival. The owls, with their highly sensitive ears, can hear most things in the forest, and lately they've been hearing a lot of human activity.

Watching the owls slip silently through the night forest, alerted to their prey only by the quiet rustling of leaves, there is no doubt of the owls' ability to listen. But watching the owl's population slip silently downwards, one is forced to wonder if we humans are capable of hearing the owls' message.

Juvenile Spotted Owls are tame and trusting
and often allow humans to approach quite closely.

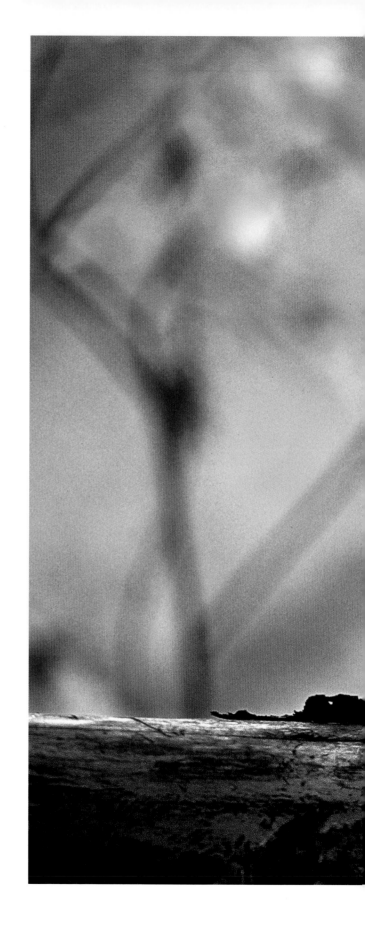

Black bears are commonly seen
in the owl's forest habitat.

When owls relax, they often fluff out their
feathers and assume a hunched position.

‹ This juvenile Mexican Spotted Owl waits
patiently after dark in anticipation of a prey
delivery from its parents.

Trees silhouetted against a moonlit night sky—
this is the world of the owl.

A juvenile Great Horned Owl calls quietly
to its parents in hopes of soliciting some food.

> Although they look like "balls of down," fledglings have well-developed flight feathers and can fly if necessary.

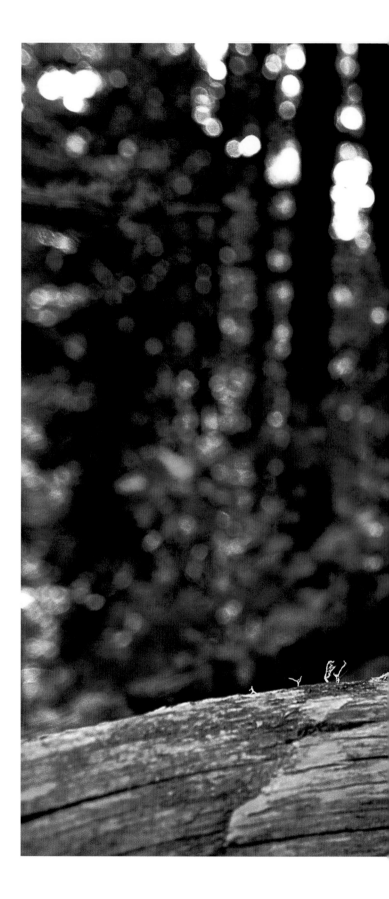

< Young owlets are more often curious than afraid.

ᵛ Young owls often spend their first months out of the nest huddling together.

⌃ Barred Owls are often found nesting and hunting in cool, damp valley bottoms along riparian areas.

› To stare into the eyes of a Spotted Owl is a privilege shared by very few people.

This "chimney nest" appears inhospitable, but inside is a soft round bed of fir needles.

‹ The Spotted Owl will always remain the
last true denizen of the old-growth forests
of western North America.

For the animal shall not be measured by man.

In a world older and more complete than ours, they move finished

and complete, gifted with the extension of the senses we

have lost or never attained, living by voices we shall never hear.

HENRY BESTON, *The Outermost House*

Acknowledgements

I wish to thank Vicky Young for her tireless support and encouragement and for her parallel understanding and appreciation of the natural world. Vicky accompanied me on many cold, dark nights, hiking through remote forests in search of owls. This book is, in so many ways, just as much a product of her labour as it is mine.

Many other biologists and technicians have accompanied me on arduous night hikes in my work as a Spotted Owl biologist; at times this work seemed like an exercise in sleep and food deprivation. I am grateful for their commitment and trust in my leadership. Among these people, both Janice Anderson and Doris Hausleitner truly stood out and greatly impressed me with their tenacity and commitment to the task and with their limitless enthusiasm and love for the natural world. I appreciate the time spent, and life lessons learned, from all of these individuals. In addition, Guy Poirier and Les Ralston spent hundreds of hours piloting my crews and me into all of the most remote valleys within the owl's range in British Columbia. Their skill as they pushed the limits of their helicopters to pick us up from some tiny cliff opening in the forest always impressed me.

Eric Forsman has been both a friend and a mentor from the very beginning of my love affair with Spotted Owls. His unwavering commitment to the science on behalf of the owls earned my respect long before I met him. It would also be inappropriate not to mention all of the other researchers and biologists who have committed their time to Spotted Owl research. Their science informed me immensely in my efforts.

Wayne Lynch continues to inspire me to better myself in my photographic pursuits, and without his mentorship this book would not exist.

Many years ago Dick Cannings opened my eyes and ultimately my ears to the wonderful world of owls. I have long appreciated his informed introduction to such a magical bird.

My parents first encouraged my photography, and my brother challenged my conservation ethic with engaging philosophical debates that served to strengthen my logic. Many friends influenced me in similar ways; their support was always appreciated.

Last, but not least, I want to thank the owls for accepting me into their mysterious and often forbidding nocturnal world. One glimpse into their eyes was always enough to motivate me to continue.

Jared Hobbs

I WOULD LIKE TO THANK Harriet Allen for introducing me to the world of Spotted Owl biology and Eric Forsman, George Barrowclough, and Susan Haig for guiding me through many of the details.

Richard Cannings

Index